Beginning and End of th
Début et Fin de la

Beginning and End of the Snow
Début et Fin de la Neige

followed by
Where the Arrow Falls

suivi de
Là où retombe la flèche

By Yves Bonnefoy
Translated by Emily Grosholz
Watercolors by Farhad Ostovani

Lewisburg
Bucknell University Press

Published by Bucknell University Press
Co-published with
The Rowman & Littlefield Publishing Group, Inc.
4501 Forbes Boulevard, Suite 200, Lanham, Maryland 20706
www.rowman.com

10 Thornbury Road, Plymouth PL6 7PP, United Kingdom

British Library Cataloguing in Publication Information Available

Library of Congress Cataloging-in-Publication Data
Library of Congress Cataloging-in-Publication Data Available
ISBN 978-1-61148-458-8 (pbk : alk. paper)

Cover Image:
Farhad Ostovani, Horizon. 23.5 x 25 cm. 2005–2006.
Water color and pastel on paper.

♾™ The paper used in this publication meets the minimum requirements
of American National Standard for Information Sciences—Permanence of
Paper for Printed Library Materials, ANSI/NISO Z39.48-1992.

Printed in the United States of America

Contents

Acknowledgements

A longer version of the essay "Song, Rain, Snow: Translating the Poetry of Yves Bonnefoy," along with the following translations from *Début et fin de la neige*, were first published in the *Hudson Review*, Vol. LXI, No. 4 (Winter 2009), pp. 618–642: From *The Great Snowfall*: "First snowfall, early this morning . . .," "The Mirror," "The Plough," "Spot of Water," "Our Lady of Mercy," "The Garden," "The Apples," "Just before dawn," *The Torches, Hopkins Forest*.

The translator would like to thank Yves and Lucie Vines Bonnefoy for their friendly consultation on the translation, as well as her son Benjamin Grosholz Edwards. She would like to thank Paula Deitz for her support as editor of the *Hudson Review* and as a friend; and Farhad Ostovani for his generous counsel on the choice of watercolors. And she would like to thank Greg Clingham and Constance Timm at Bucknell University Press, Brooke Bascietto at Rowman & Littlefield, and Catherine Farin and Isabelle Gallimard at Mercure de France for their cooperation, insight, and skill in the preparation of this book.

The Preface, "Snow in French and English," was written by Yves Bonnefoy for this volume, and has not been published before in French or English.

Preface

Yves Bonnefoy

"Snow in French and English"
Translated by Emily Grosholz

Does snow fall the same way in every language? Perhaps, for
that to be the case, the words of each language would have to
have the same relations: the same ways of meeting, of melting
into or avoiding each other, of making great whirlwinds or easy
somersaults, minutes of agitation followed by instants when the
sky seems to be immobile, after which sudden lights appear. And
since that can't be the case, perhaps, since the idioms that divide
up the earth are so various, it seems probable that our diverse
cultures never have altogether the same snows. It snows the way
we talk. We watch the snow fall at this level in our speech where
the flake whose flight we follow, gracefully hesitating between
increase (interlocking with others) and dissipation (soon enough
becoming not much more than light), makes us divide ourselves
between dream and knowledge, hesitating between the words of
desiring imagination and those of conceptual thought. And those
are then moments or myths, inventions of each way of speaking,
illusions of all of them, which occur in order to distract us from
the evidence, from what is only evident. Each language has its
own idea of snow.

I ask myself this question. These perceptions of snow which
are thus disparate and may even be hardly compatible—snow
as experienced in the Himalayas by a Tibetan monk, almost
barefoot, as opposed to snow for our children at play, all bundled

up in heavy clothing—perhaps sometimes they touch upon each other. Don't they have the same sort of relation that snowflakes have—quite vivid, one would say with confidence—snowflakes thrown together by a shadow of wind, in an instant of light? And how does it stand then with French and English, these two languages that have mingled their words during so many eras in their history, and often to express the same thought, or almost? One and the same, since from Massachusetts to Wales to the Limousin, snow falls on very similar fields and woods. Except, it's true, that the houses of these diverse countries may be very different. In our French countryside, buildings of heavy stone with narrow windows, dark rooms where the cold outside only enters for a moment when the door is opened, after which reality returns, first and foremost the fire that one hears on the hearth. And in New England, those light constructions of resonant wood, where so often vases full of bright flowers are placed behind the window-panes.

And what about *snow* in the exchanges between English and French? Alas, I fear that for translators our perceptions of almost anything (in the language that Shakespeare unified, and the language that for so many years obsessed Racine) have acquired particular features that are often irreducible. So I fear that Emily Grosholz, translating *Début et fin de la neige*, found it rather difficult to locate certain points of view in French within the field of the English language, so much more more aptly fashioned than my own for the observation of concrete detail at a specific place and time, otherwise put, for the expression of the events of a particular existence.

French lacks a stressed accent. This gives each one of our words in relation to others in the same line a kind of autonomy. An English word, since it is inherently accented, carries in itself a rhythm, thanks to which—without ceasing to speak of the closest and simplest realities—it can unite with other words in a naturally iambic line, where the relations between things and feelings that poetry reveals have not lost contact with everyday life. A French word, in itself, has no accent. As such, it can't bestow any rhythm; it doesn't register its own aptness for song, but seems by contrast ready for conversation, debate, the analysis of thought, all activities that turn us away from noticing a tree or listening to a bird sing. In order to integrate a French word into the schema of a simple form, which alone will save it from being just a concept, the poet must handle it in terms of its 'external' feature, the number of its syllables. Only thus is the word able, if not to forget its original, habitual meaning, at least to transgress or transfigure it, to make it the instrument of metaphysical research. Indeed, the French word reminds me of snow. But is it the same that falls, dear Emily, in your poems, or in those of other English-speaking poets?

Whose woods these are, I think I know—

In this poem by Robert Frost, "Stopping by Woods on a Snowy Evening," the accentual stresses are resolutely asserted from the very first line; they make the tetrameter possible, four iambic feet, as strongly imprinted in the verbal subject matter as footprints on a deep layer of fresh snow. From the very beginning, thanks to the rhythm, we are in the midst of a poem. But what does Frost do then? He reflects, as does every great poet, on the sky, the earth, God, people. But, if we believe certain interpretations of his poem, he is no less the country doctor who goes around from house to house visiting his patients, in the countryside he knows so well, and he looks out on these roads and woods just as those to whom he attends look out. From all of this arises a meaning that is thoroughly social—private property, the right to till the land, legal disputes that may follow between neighbors—which suggests to him the metaphor he uses as a poet to talk about God, whose woods these are. Whose woods these are, literally, he knows perfectly well, someone "whose house is in the village —" But beside the house of the pharmacist, or the grocer, there is the house of God in red brick, next to the other, wooden houses, where one hears the singing of hymns rise up on Sundays.

In French poetry, we just don't have that easy continuity between the ultimate ends and the most immediate social reality "in the village." As for my own snow, I was happy to think that one might call it *e muets dans une phrase*, "silent e's in a sentence." In the folds of the snow that falls so thick and fast, I am not going to find myself, right away, on Main Street, because they lead me rather to brood over the depths of my own language where it is only apropos human nature in all its generality that the questions (over which my poetry labors) are posed. Are we really only forms of matter? The words dearest to us, must we then take them to be haphazard movements in sentences without truth, like atoms in the universe of Lucretius? Or is there with them, or behind them, someone of interest to us? It is the duty of our French snow to forget that it is only snow, on this road right here, this morning, in order better to offer us the great meanings or signifiers that answer to the great questions it recalls. My snow is a letter that I receive. But its flakes whirl, its words disperse and fade: the letter can no longer be deciphered.

Reading Emily Grosholz's translation, I re-read my own poems and something strikes me. In *Début et fin de la neige*, the same comparison recurs quite often, from the first pages which assemble the most immediate perceptions, to the final reflection at the end, "The Only Rose." It is that snowflakes are words, words—in a letter or poem—are falling snow, and there are relations in our speech that resemble encounters that reunite and then sunder the flakes. As if snow were language, language snow.

And then I ask, what does this comparison mean? Is it just

a whim of the imagination, or does it have, in its dream idiom, a reason for being? I'd like to pose this question more seriously, one time or another, although the snowflakes of my metaphor, dancing while they laugh (as is their custom), never fail to make fun of my excess, or defect, of philosophy.

Just a remark, which is only prudential. If snowflakes make us think of words, and words of snowflakes, this certainly doesn't happen when we see in words only the concepts that produce science or determine many of our actions: stripped of wings, these semantic bits fall too heavily under their counter-natural burden of meaning: soon they will turn into rain and one day or another into a flood from which humanity may never emerge.

The snowflake in the word—it occurs when we take vocables or verbs—or even conjunctions, even periods or colons, even commas—with all their sonorities, their colors, their dishevelments, their syncopations—those silent e's. And this metaphor that I have dreamed up, it speaks of poems, only poems. Fine! But if poems resemble snowfalls, don't I have to infer that the better we observe snow, the better we can understand poetry, what it is, or what we would like it to be?

Can we do it? Can I really come up with an idea, in terms of the falling snow, of what a poem desires? Yes, and first and foremost, that desire is to fragment, undo, dissipate, the articulation of concepts. Snowflakes have too many dimensions, unpredicted and unpredictable, to make us think about rationality in discourse. To compare snow and speech is to refuse the truth of mathematical formula and practical intent; the truth of speech is much vaster and more like dancing.

But it is also, I believe, to desire much more. Far beyond the conceptual articulations that characterize our ordinary speech, in the upriver distances of language, exist the structures of syntax that obey the principles of logic, non-contradiction and excluded middle. These syntactic structures organize the reciprocal relations among the objects of our thought, but also and above all the relations among aspects and impulses of life. And that guidance and control of syntax over our existence is certainly very beautiful and reassuring, because it allows us, by organizing our actions, to make of this moment of life, our finitude, a place on earth where we can encounter other beings. To establish ourselves on this narrow walkway with the deep, plunging perspective out over that which we can thereafter understand as One, and being, not as elsewhere, as nothing.

Yes, but . . . Shouldn't we be a bit surprised that syntax exhibits differences, from one language to another? This language has an aorist, that one doesn't. These languages have declensions, while those have simplified declensions and those none at all. And without being an expert in linguistics, I suppose that other disparities appear with respect to languages (wrongly) called archaic or primitive, which are more subtle but perhaps more important, like cracks in the inner walls of our ways of seeing . . . All our human syntaxes, aren't they just relative forms, each one unsatisfying with respect to another, higher up in the ascent of spirit? A higher syntax that would stand with respect to all the others as non-Euclidean geometries do, at the outer boundary of our natural understanding? One that, in its intelligence apropos being, might be more like—fastening and unfastening its forms in the light—those snowflakes that we see at the very top of the sky, in the blue that envelops worlds? Syntax of the One still in-itself, hardly unfurled, already however all things. The same intuition, it seems to me, that Petrarch had when he entered with great happiness, one bright morning of the soul, into the scattering of thousands of rose petals.

But let's not dream like this. Let's stay with our snow of here and now, which we don't chase through the sky but watch as it lives near the ground, on branches, on a garden bench, on a plank of wood left leaning against a wall that makes a vivid patch of color against its whiteness. This snow, which is so quick to cover up again a barn left naked between two snowdrifts, with a red prior to words. The snow that follows us from one place to another, on certain days or nights, as in the poem by Robert Frost.

And a few words, to come back to the poems which Emily Grosholz has translated, since they sometimes require a certain explication. Hopkins Forest is a real place, as my walks in that beautiful forest were real. They stretched out over a period of months, long months, summer, autumn, winter, in Williamstown, Massachusetts, a sojourn that gave rise among other things to this whole book. In Williamstown, I learned what snow is. I'd often encountered it when I lived in Cambridge, Massachusetts, or New York, but of course that was always in a city, where the snow was prevented from expressing all its thoughts because it had been shovelled into heaps and soiled, and so left without relation to the trees and animals. I had to live in a small village next to the great forest.

But the portrait of Baudelaire was also real. I really saw the open newspaper with his enormous picture, for a moment, on the train. And if I dreamed that instant, in any case it was so immediate and so strong that later on I never found any reason to doubt it. Baudelaire has the same reality as Hopkins Forest, and so he is written into the poem with the same level of meaning.

As for "The Only Rose," it also belongs here. The grid thrown down by the snow that winter over the world allowed me, in virtue of those days, to see and understand better situations and things which earlier in my life I'd dearly loved: small woods of pine and oak in Haute Provence, building façades and rooms designed by Alberti, by San Gallo, by Palladio, those architects who seem to haunt the same sky-blue, the same blue sky, from which the snow must fall.

La Grande Neige

The Great Snowfall

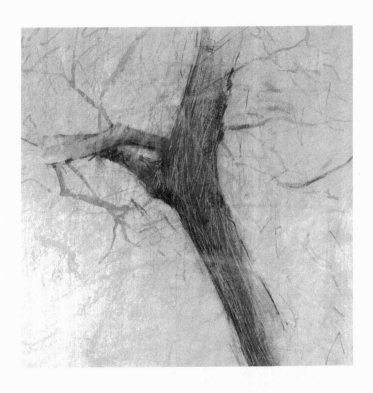

Farhad Ostovani, White Mulberry. 30 x 30 cm. 2006.
Water color, pastel and pencil on paper.

[Sans titre]

Première neige tôt ce matin. L'ocre, le vert
Se réfugient sous les arbres.

Seconde, vers midi. Ne demeure
De la couleur
Que les aiguilles de pins
Qui tombent elles aussi plus dru parfois que la neige.

Puis, vers le soir,
Le fléau de la lumière s'immobilise.
Les ombres et les rêves ont même poids.

Un peu de vent
Écrit du bout du pied un mot hors du monde.

[Untitled]

First snowfall, early this morning. Ochre, green
Huddle under the trees.

The second, towards noon. Nothing
Is left of color
But needles from the pines
Falling sometimes thicker than snow.

Then, towards evening,
The light stands poised.
Shadows and dreams balance on the scales.

A faint wind
Writes in the snow a word beyond the world.

Le miroir

Hier encore
Les nuages passaient
Au fond noir de la chambre.
Mais à présent le miroir est vide.

Neiger
Se désenchevêtre du ciel.

The Mirror

Yesterday still
The clouds sailed across
The dark end of the room,
But now the mirror's empty.

Snow
Disentangles from the sky.

La charrue

Cinq heures. La neige encore. J'entends des voix
À l'avant du monde.

Une charrue
Comme une lune au troisième quartier
Brille, mais la recouvre
La nuit d'un pli de la neige.

Et cet enfant
A toute la maison pour lui, désormais. Il va
D'une fenêtre à l'autre. Il presse
Ses doigts contre la vitre. Il voit
Des gouttes se former là où il cesse
D'en pousser la buée vers le ciel qui tombe.

The Plough

Five o'clock. More snow. I hear some voices
At the edge of the world.

A plough
Like a three-quarter moon
Shines, but then is covered
By the darkness of a fold of snow.

And from now on that child
Has the house all to himself. He goes
From one window to another. He presses
His fingers against the misted pane. He sees
Drops forming where his fingertips stop
Pushing the condensation towards the sky that falls.

Le peu d'eau

À ce flocon
Qui sur ma main se pose, j'ai désir
D'assurer l'éternel
En faisant de ma vie, de ma chaleur,
De mon passé, de ces jours d'à présent,
Un instant simplement: cet instant-ci, sans bornes.

Mais déjà il n'est plus
Qu'un peu d'eau, qui se perd
Dans la brume des corps qui vont dans la neige

Spot of Water

To the snowflake
Poised on my hand, I would
Grant eternity,
Understanding my life, my warmth,
My past, these current days,
As simply a moment, this one, limitless.

And yet it melts: already
Only a spot of water, strayed
Into the mist of bodies moving through the snow.

[Sans titre]

Neige
Fugace sur l'écharpe, sur le gant
Comme cette illusion, le coquelicot,
Dans la main qui rêva, l'été passé
Sur le chemin parmi les pierres sèches,
Que l'absolu est à portée du monde.

Pourtant, quelle promesse
Dans cette eau, de contact léger, puisqu'elle fut,
Un instant, la lumière! Le ciel d'été
N'a guère de nuées pour entrouvrir
Plus clair chemin sous des voûtes plus sombres.

Circé
Sous sa pergola d'ombres, l'illuminée,
N'eut pas de fruits plus rouges.

[Untitled]

Snow
Fugitive on the scarf, the glove
Like that illusion, coquelicot,
In the hand that dreamt, last summer
On a path among dry stones,
That the absolute lies within reach of the world.

All the same, what promise
In this drop of water, this brief touch, since it was
Just for a moment, light! No riven cloud
Of a summer sky could open to reveal
A clearer path underneath darker vaults.

Circe
Under her pergola of shadows, the enlightened,
Had no fruits redder than these.

La vierge de miséricorde

Tout, maintenant,
Bien au chaud
Sous ton manteau léger,
Presque rien que de brume et de broderie,
Madone de miséricorde de la neige.

Contre ton corps
Dorment, nus,
Les êtres et les choses, et tes doigts
Voilent de leur clarté ces paupières closes.

Our Lady of Mercy

Everything, now,
Gathers in warmth
Under your light mantle,
Barely more than mist and knotted lace,
Lady of Mercy of the snow.

Against your body
Creatures and things,
Naked, lie fast asleep, and your fingers
With their clarity veil those closed eyelids.

Le jardin

Il neige.
Sous les flocons la porte
Ouvre enfin au jardin
De plus que le monde.

J'avance. Mais se prend
Mon écharpe à du fer
Rouillé, et se déchire
En moi l'étoffe du songe.

The Garden

It's snowing.
Beneath the snowflakes the gate
Opens at last on the garden
Of more than the world.

I enter. But my scarf
Catches on rusty iron,
And it tears apart in me
The fabric of the dream.

Farhad Ostovani, Horizon. 23.5 x 25 cm. 2005-2006.
Water color and pastel on paper.

Les pommes

Et que faut-il penser
De ces pommes jaunes?
Hier, elles étonnaient, d'attendre ainsi, nues
Après la chute des feuilles,

Aujourd'hui elles charment
Tant leurs épaules
Sont, modestement, soulignées
D'un ourlet de neige.

The Apples

And what should one think
Of these yellow apples? Yesterday,
They surprised us, waiting that way, naked
After the fall of leaves.

Today they charm,
So modestly their shoulders
Are traced
By a scallop of snow.

L'eté encore

J'avance dans la neige, j'ai fermé
Les yeux, mais la lumière sait franchir
Les paupières poreuses, et je perçois
Que dans mes mots c'est encore la neige
Qui tourbillonne, se resserre, se déchire.

Neige,
Lettre que l'on retrouve et que l'on déplie,
Et l'encre en a blanchi et dans les signes
La gaucherie de l'esprit est visible
Qui ne sait qu'enchevêtrer les ombres claires.

Et on essaye de lire, on ne comprend pas
Qui s'intéresse à nous dans la mémoire,
Sinon que c'est l'été encore; et que l'on voit
Sous les flocons les feuilles, et la chaleur
Monter du sol absent comme une brume.

Still Summer

I am walking into the snow, I closed
My eyes, but light can penetrate
Porous eyelids, and I see
That even in my words the snow whirls,
Gathers, tears itself apart.

Snow,
A letter rediscovered and unfolded,
Whose ink has faded and whose characters
Display the awkwardness of mind
That can only tangle their clear shadows.

And we try to read, we don't know who
Would think to write to us in memory,
Except that it's still summer; and that we see
Leaves beneath the snowflakes, and warmth
Rising from the absent soil like mist.

[Sans titre]

On dirait beaucoup d'e muets dans une phrase.
On sent qu'on ne leur doit
Que des ombres de métaphores.

On dirait,
Dès qu'il neige plus dru,
De ces mains qui repoussent d'autres mains

Mais jouent avec les doigts qu'elles refusent.

[Untitled]

One might say, a flurry of silent e's inside a sentence.
We sense that nothing's owed to them
But shadows of metaphors.

One might say,
As the snow flies thicker,
It's like hands that thrust back other hands

But play with the very fingers they refuse.

[Sans titre]

Flocons,
Bévues sans conséquences de la lumière.
L'une suit l'autre et d'autres encore, comme si
Comprendre ne comptait plus, rire advantage.

Et Aristote le disait bien,
Quelque part dans sa *Poétique* qu'on lit si mal,
C'est la transparence qui vaut,
Dans des phrases qui soient comme une rumeur
      d'abeilles, comme une eau claire.

[Untitled]

Snowflakes,
Inconsequential mistakes of light.
One follows on another, on others still, as if
Understanding no longer counted, only laughter.

And Aristotle said it well,
Somewhere in the *Poetics* that we read so poorly,
Transparence is what matters,
In sentences that should be like the rumor
    of bees, or like clear water.

De natura rerum

Lucrèce le savait:
Ouvre le coffre,
Tu verras, il est plein de neige
Qui tourbillonne.

Et parfois deux flocons
Se rencontrent, s'unissent,
Ou bien l'un se détourne, gracieusement
Dans son peu de mort.

D'où vient qu'il fasse clair
Dans quelques mots
Quand l'un n'est que la nuit,
L'autre, qu'un rêve?

D'où viennent ces deux ombres
Qui vont, riant,
Et l'une emmitouflée
D'une laine rouge?

De Natura Rerum

Lucretius knew it:
Open the box,
You'll see, it's full of snow
In flux, aswirl.

And sometimes two flakes
Meet, unite,
Or else one swerves, gently
In its slight death.

How is it, that in some words
Daylight occurs,
When one is only night,
The other, dream?

Where do they come from,
These two shadows
Who walk off laughing, one
In red wool coat and mittens?

La parure

Il neige. Âme, que voulais-tu
Que tu n'aies eu de naissance éternelle?
Vois, tu as là
Pour la mort même une robe de fête?

Une parure comme à l'adolescence,
De celles que l'on prend à mains soucieuses
Car l'étoffe en est transparente et reste près
Des doigts qui la déploient dans la lumière,
On sait qu'elle est fragile comme l'amour.

Mais des corolles, des feuilles y sont brodées,
Et déjà la musique se fait entendre
Dans la salle voisine, illuminée.
Une ardeur mystérieuse te prend la main.

The Gown

It's snowing. Soul, what were you wishing for
That you did not possess eternally?
Look, there you have
An evening gown for the occasion, death.

One of those gowns for adolescent girls,
That we take delicately in hand
Because the fine material's transparent, gathered
Against the fingers that unfold it in the light;
Like love, we know it's fragile.

But wreathes and foliage are embroidered over it,
And in another, brightly lighted room
Music has already started.
A mysterious ardor takes you by the hand,

You walk, heart pounding, into the great snow.

Noli me tangere

Hésite le flocon dans le ciel bleu
À nouveau, le dernier flocon de la grande neige.

Et c'est comme entrerait au jardin celle qui
Avait bien dû rêver ce qui pourrait être,
Ce regard, ce dieu simple, sans souvenir
Du tombeau, sans pensée que le bonheur,
Sans avenir
Que sa dissipation dans le bleu du monde.

«Non, ne me touche pas,» lui dirait-il,
Mais même dire non serait de lumière.

Noli me tangere

It hesitates, the snowflake in the sky turned blue
Again, anew, the last flake of the great snow.

And it's as if she'd come into the garden,
She who must have dreamed what might be so,
That look, that plain god, with no memory
Of the tomb, with no thought but happiness,
With no future
Except his long dispersal into the world's blue.

"No, do not touch me," he might say to her,
But even his saying no would become light.

[Sans titre]

Juste avant l'aube
Je regarde à travers les vitres, et je crois comprendre
Qu'il a cessé de neiger. Une flaque bleue
S'étend, brillante un peu, devant les arbres,
D'une paroi à l'autre de la nuit.

Je sors.
Je descends précautionneusement l'escalier de bois
Dont les marches sont nivelées par la neige fraîche.
Le froid cerne et pénètre mes chevilles,
Il semble que l'esprit en soit plus clair,
Qui perçoit mieux le silence des choses.

Dort-il encore
Dans l'enchevêtrement du tas de bois
Serré sous la fenêtre,
Le chipmunk, notre voisin simple,
Ou est-il déjà à errer dans les crissements et le froid?
Je vois d'infimes marques devant la porte.

[Untitled]

Just before dawn,
I look out past the windowpane, and understand
That it's stopped snowing. A small blue pool
Spreads out, shining a bit, in front of the trees,
From one wall to the other of night's enclosure.

I step outside.
Cautiously, I descend the wooden staircase
Whose steps are heaped level with fresh snow.
The cold surrounds and sinks into my ankles,
It seems as if cold clarifies the spirit,
Which better appreciates the muteness of things.

Is he still sleeping
In the tangle of the woodpile
Stacked up under the window,
The chipmunk, our plain neighbor,
Or is he already up, scrabbling in the cold?
I see some tiny prints before the door.

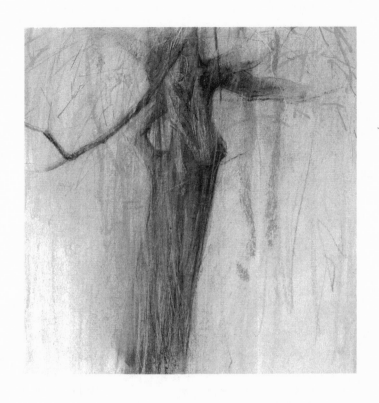

Farhad Ostovani, White Mulberry. 30 x 30 cm. 2006.
Water color, pastel and pencil on paper.

Les flambeaux

Neige
Qui as cessé de donner, qui n'es plus
Celle qui vient mais celle qui attend
En silence, ayant apporté mais sans qu'encore
On ait pris, et pourtant, toute la nuit,
Nous avons aperçu, dans l'embuement
Des vitres parfois mêmes ruisselantes,
Ton étincellement sur la grande table.

Neige, notre chemin,
Immaculé encore, pour aller prendre
Sous les branches courbées et comme attentives
Ces flambeaux, ce qui est, qui ont paru
Un à un, et brûlé, mais semblent s'éteindre
Comme aux yeux du désir quand il accède
Aux biens dont il rêvait (car c'est souvent
Quand tout se dénouerait peut-être, que s'efface
En nous de salle en salle le reflet
Du ciel, dans les miroirs), ô neige, touche

The Torches

Snow,
Which has ceased to give, which is no longer
The one who comes, but rather waits
In silence, having brought what none
Has yet taken up, and still, all night long,
We glimpsed, through misted windows,
Even sometimes streaming,
Your glittering across the great expanse.

Snow, our path,
Still immaculate, where we may go to take up
Under the branches, curved and as if waiting,
These torches—what exists—which one by one
Appeared, and burned, but seemed to fade
Like the eyes of desire when it gains
The gifts it dreamed of (for it often happens
When all could be perhaps resolved, that the reflection
Of the sky, in mirrors, dims
In us, from room to room), o snow, touch

Encore ces flambeaux, renflamme-les
Dans le froid de cette aube ; et qu'à l'exemple
De tes flocons qui déjà les assaillent
De leur insouciance, feu plus clair,
Et malgré tant de fièvre dans la parole
Et tant de nostalgie dans le souvenir,
Nos mots ne cherchent plus les autres mots mais les avoisinent,
Passent auprès d'eux, simplement,
Et si l'un en a frôlé un, et s'ils s'unissent,
Ce ne sera qu'encore ta lumière,
Notre brièveté qui se dissémine,
L'écriture qui se dissipe, sa tâche faite.

(Et tel flocon s'attarde, on le suit des yeux,
On aimerait le regarder toujours,
Tel autre s'est posé sur la main offerte.

Et tel plus lent et comme égaré s'éloigne
Et tournoie, puis revient. Et n'est-ce dire
Qu'un mot, un autre mot encore, à inventer,
Rédimerait le monde ? Mais on ne sait
Si on entend ce mot ou si on le rêve).

The torches again, rekindle them
In the chill of this dawn; and by the example
Of your flakes that already assail them
With their lightheartedness, clearer fire,
In spite of so much fever in our speech
And so much homesickness in memory,
Our words no longer seek out other words, but live nearby
Passing beside them, simply,
And if one grazes another, and if they merge,
It will still be only your light,
Our transience that disperses,
Writing that vanishes, its task done.

(And a snowflake lingers, our eyes follow it,
We'd like to watch it forever,
Another poises on the open hand.

And another, slower and as if lost, recedes
And whirls, then returns. And isn't that to say
One word, then another word, to be invented,
Might redeem the world? Yet we don't know
If we understand this word, or dream it.)

Farhad Ostovani, Horizon. 23.5 x 25 cm. 2005 -2006.
Water color and pastel on paper.

Hopkins Forest

J'étais sorti
Prendre de l'eau au puits, auprès des arbres,
Et je fus en présence d'un autre ciel.
Disparues les constellations d'il y a un instant encore,
Les trois quarts du firmament étaient vides,
Le noir le plus intense y régnait seul,
Mais à gauche, au-dessus de l'horizon,
Mêlé à la cime des chênes,
Il y a avait un amas d'étoiles rougeoyantes
Comme un brasier, d'où montait même une fumée.

Je rentrai
Et je rouvris le livre sur la table.
Page après page,
Ce n'étaient que des signes indéchiffrables,
Des agrégats de formes d'aucun sens
Bien que vaguement récurrentes,
Et par-dessous une blancheur d'abîme
Comme si ce qu'on nomme l'esprit tombait là, sans bruit,
Comme une neige.
Je tournai cependant les pages.

Hopkins Forest

I went outside
To draw some water from the well, beside the trees,
And I was in the presence of another sky.
Gone the constellations of a moment before,
Three quarters of the firmament were empty,
The deepest blackness alone held sway there,
Except that on the left, above the horizon,
Mixed in the crown of trees,
There was a mass of glowing stars
Like a brazier, from which a coil of smoke arose.

I went inside
And re-opened the book upon the table.
Page after page,
There were only indecipherable signs,
Aggregates of forms that made no sense
Despite their vague recurrence,
And underneath a whiteness, an abyss
As if what we call spirit were falling there,
Quietly, like snow.
Nonetheless, I turned the pages.

Bien des années plus tôt,
Dans un train au moment où le jour se lève
Entre Princeton Junction et Newark,
C'est-à-dire deux lieux de hasard pour moi,
Deux retombées des flèches de nulle part,
Les voyageurs lisaient, silencieux
Dans la neige qui balayait les vitres grises,
Et soudain,
Dans un journal ouvert à deux pas de moi,
Une grande photographie de Baudelaire,
Toute un page
Comme le ciel se vide à la fin du monde
Pour consentir au désordre des mots.

J'ai rapproché ce rêve et ce souvenir
Quand j'ai marché, d'abord tout un automne
Dans des bois où bientôt ce fut la neige
Qui triompha, dans beaucoup de ces signes
Que l'on reçoit, contradictoirement,
Du monde dévasté par le langage.
Prenait fin le conflit de deux principes,
Me semblait-il, se mêlaient deux lumières,
Se refermaient les lèvres de la plaie.
La masse blanche du froid tombait par rafales
Sur la couleur, mais un toit au loin, une planche
Peinte, restée debout contre une grille,
C'était encore la couleur, et mystérieuse
Comme un qui sortirait du sépulcre et, riant:
« Non, ne me touche pas », dirait-il au monde.

Many years before,
On a train at dawn
Between Princeton Junction and Newark,
That's to say, for me two accidental places,
Where two arrows from nowhere happened to fall,
The travellers were reading, silent
In the snowfall that swept the gray train windows.
And suddenly,
In an open newspaper one seat over,
A big photograph of Baudelaire,
A whole page
As if the sky emptied at the end of the world
In order to consent to the disorder of words.

I compared this dream and this memory
As I walked, at first throughout an autumn
In woods where soon enough the snow
Triumphed, in many of those signs
That we receive, contradictory,
From a world devastated by language.
The conflict of two principles resolved,
It seemed to me, two lights commingled.
The edges of the wound were closed.
The white mass of the cold fell in great heaps
Over color, except for a distant roof, a painted
Plank, set up against a fence,
There was still color, as mysterious
As he who might have walked out of the tomb and,
        laughing,
Said "No, don't touch me," to the world.

Je dois vraiment beaucoup à Hopkins Forest,
Je la garde à mon horizon, dans sa partie
Qui quitte le visible pour l'invisible
Par le tressaillement du bleu des lointains.
Je l'écoute, à travers les bruits, et parfois même,
L'été, poussant du pied les feuilles mortes
D'autres années, claires dans la pénombre
Des chênes trop serrés parmi les pierres,
Je m'arrête, je crois que ce sol s'ouvre
À l'infini, que ces feuilles y tombent
Sans hâte, ou bien remontent, le haut, le bas
N'étant plus, ni le bruit, sauf le léger
Chuchotement des flocons qui bientôt
Se multiplient, se rapprochent, se nouent
– Et je revois alors tout l'autre ciel,
J'entre pour un instant dans la grande neige.

Truly, I owe much to Hopkins Forest.
I keep it on my horizon, along the line
That abandons the visible for the invisible
Where the blue of distance shimmers.
I hear it, across other sounds, and even sometimes,
In summer, pushing my feet through dead leaves from
Other years, pale in the shadow
Of oak trees crowded together among the stones,
I stop, I think the ground has opened
Onto the infinite, that these leaves fall here
Unhurrying, or indeed mount, for high and low
No longer exist, nor sound, except for the soft
Whispering of snowflakes, that soon
Multiply, draw near together, knot.
—And I see then that other sky,
I enter for a moment into the great snow.

47

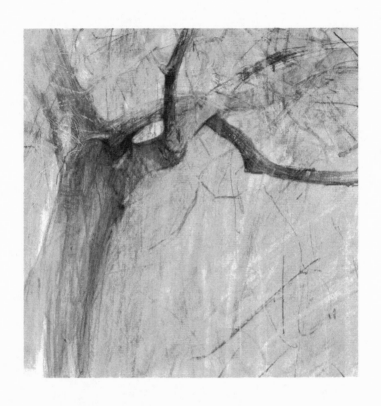

Farhad Ostovani, White Mulberry. 30 x 30 cm. 2006.
Water color, pastel and pencil on paper.

Le tout, le rien

I

C'est la dernière neige de la saison,
La neige de printemps, la plus habile
À recoudre les déchirures du bois mort
Avant qu'on ne l'emporte puis le brûle.

C'est la première neige de ta vie
Puisque, hier, ce n'étaient encore que des taches
De couleur, plaisirs brefs, craintes, chagrins
Inconsistants, faute de la parole.

Et je vois que la joie prend sur la peur
Dans tes yeux que dessille la surprise
Une avance, d'un grand bon clair : ce cri, ce rire
Que j'aime, et que je trouve méditable.

Car nous sommes bien proches, et l'enfant
Est le progéniteur de qui l'a pris
Un matin dans ses mains d'adulte et soulevé
Dans le consentement de la lumière.

Everything, Nothing

I.

It is the last snow of the season,
The snow of springtime, which is most adept
At stitching up rifts in the dry wood
Before we bring it inside for the fire.

It is the first snow of your life
Since, yesterday, there were no more than
Patches of color, fugitive pleasures, fears,
Inconsistent sorrows, unheld by speech.

And now I see that joy overtakes fear
In your eyes, startled wide by astonishment,
An advance, by one clear leap: that cry, that laughter,
Which I love, where I find food for thought.

For we are close indeed, and the child
Is parent to the man who grasped her
One morning in his grown-up hands,
And lifted her to the willingness of the light.

II

Oui, à entendre, oui, à faire mienne
Cette source, le cri de joie, qui bouillonnante
Surgit d'entre les pierres de la vie
Tôt, et si fort, puis faiblit et s'aveugle.

Mais écrire n'est pas avoir, ce n'est pas être,
Car le tressaillement de la joie n'y est
Qu'une ombre, serait-elle la plus claire,
Dans des mots qui encore se souviennent

De tant et tant de choses que le temps
A durement labourées de ses griffes,
– Et je ne puis donc faire que te dire
Ce que je ne suis pas, sauf en désir.

Une façon de prendre, qui serait
De cesser d'être soi dans l'acte de prendre,
Une façon de dire, qui ferait
Qu'on ne serait plus seul dans le langage.

II.

Yes, hear and understand, and make my own
That spring, the cry of joy which, bubbling up,
Suddenly rises among the stones of life,
Early and so strongly, then slackens and falls blind.

But to write is not to have, it is not being,
Since the trembling start of joy is there in it
Only as shadow, though the most luminous,
In words that still remember

So many... so many things, that time
Has cruelly worked over with its claws.
—And so I can do nothing more than tell you
What I am not, except in wanting.

A way of grasping, which would be
To cease to be oneself while grasping,
A way of speaking, whose effect would be
No longer to be left alone in language.

III

Te soit la grande neige le tout, le rien,
Enfant des premiers pas titubants dans l'herbe,
Les yeux encore pleins de l'origine,
Les mains ne s'agrippant qu'à la lumière.

Te soient ces branches qui scintillent la parole
Que tu dois écouter mais sans comprendre
Le sens de leur découpe sur le ciel,
Sinon tu ne dénommerais qu'au prix de perdre.

Te suffisent les deux valeurs, l'une brillante,
De la colline dans l'échancrure des arbres,
Abeille de la vie, quand se tarira
Dans ton rêve du monde ce monde même.

Et que l'eau qui ruisselle dans le pré
Te montre que la joie peut survivre au rêve
Quand la brise d'on ne sait où venue déjà disperse
Les fleurs de l'amandier, pourtant l'autre neige.

III.

For you, let the great snow be everything, nothing,
Child of first steps unsteady in the grass,
Your eyes still welling with the origin,
Your hands clinging only to the light.

For you, let these glistening branches be the word
That you must hear, but without understanding
The meaning of their outline on the sky,
For otherwise what you would name, you'll lose.

For you, let those two values be enough, one
Shining on the hillside among trees,
Bee of life, when in your dream of the world
The world itself will finally fall silent.

And let the brook that tumbles in the meadow
Show you that joy may survive the dream,
When the breeze from who knows where scatters
The flowers of the almond tree, another snowfall.

Farhad Ostovani, Horizon. 23.5 x 25 cm. 2005-2006.
Water color and pastel on paper.

La seule rose

I

Il neige, c'est revenir dans une ville
Où, et je le découvre en avançant
Au hasard dans des rues qui toutes sont vides,
J'aurais vécu heureux une autre enfance.
Sous les flocons j'aperçois des façades
Qui ont beauté plus que rien de ce monde.
Seuls parmi nous Alberti puis San Gallo
À San Biagio, dans la salle la plus intense
Qu'ait bâtie le désir, ont approché
De cette perfection, de cette absence.

Et je regarde donc, avidement,
Ces masses que la neige me dérobe.
Je recherche surtout, dans la blancheur
Errante, ces frontons que je vois qui montent
À un plus haut niveau de l'apparence.
Ils déchirent la brume, c'est comme si
D'une main délivrée de la pesanteur
L'architecte d'ici avait fait vivre
D'un seul grand trait floral
La forme que voulait de siècle en siècle
La douleur d'être né dans la matière

The Only Rose

I.
It's snowing, that takes me back to a city
Where, and I discover it by wandering
Through streets that are all empty,
I might have spent a happy childhood.
Under the snowflakes I study the façades
More beautiful than anything in this world.
Among us, only Alberti and then San Gallo
At San Biagio, in that room—the most intense
Desire ever constructed—has approached
That perfection, that absence.

And so I watch, eagerly,
These masses that the snow hides from me.
Above all, I seek out in the errant
Whiteness, these façades that I see, which rise
To a higher level of appearance.
They tear the mist aside, it's as if
With a hand freed from gravity
The architect of this place had brought alive
With a single great floral gesture
The form that, century to century,
The grief of being born into matter, wished for.

II

Et là-haut je ne sais si c'est la vie
Encore, ou la joie seule, qui se détache
Sur ce ciel qui n'est plus de notre monde.
Ô bâtisseurs
Non tant d'un lieu que d'un regain de l'espérance,
Qu'y a-t-il au secret de ces parois
Qui devant moi s'écartent ? Ce que je vois
Le long des murs, ce sont des niches vides,
Des pleins et des déliés, d'où s'évapore
Par la grâce des nombres
Le poids de la naissance dans l'exil,
Mais de la neige s'y est mise et s'y entasse,
Je m'approche de l'une d'elles, la plus basse,
Je fais tomber un peu de sa lumière,
Et soudain c'est le pré de mes dix ans,
Les abeilles bourdonnent,
Ce que j'ai dans mes mains, ces fleurs, ces ombres,
Est-ce presque du miel, est-ce de la neige ?

II.

And high above I don't know whether it's life
Still, or only joy, that is released
Under this sky no longer of our world.
O builders,
Not so much of a place as of hope's revival,
What is the secret of these inner walls
That open before me? What I see
Along the walls, some solid and some thinner,
Are empty niches, from which evaporates
By the grace of numbers
The burden of birth in exile,
But some of the snow begins to heap up there,
I draw near to one of them, the lowest,
I tip out a bit of its light,
And suddenly it's the meadow of my tenth year,
The bees go about humming,
What I have in my hands, these flowers, these shadows,
Is it almost honey, is it snow?

III

J'avance alors, jusque sous l'arche d'une porte.
Les flocons tourbillonnent, effaçant
La limite entre les dehors et cette salle
Où des lampes sont allumées : mais elles-mêmes
Une sorte de neige, qui hésite
Entre le haut, le bas, dans cette nuit.
C'est comme si j'étais sur un second seuil.

Et au-delà ce même bruit d'abeilles
Dans le bruit de la neige. Ce que disaient
Les abeilles sans nombre de l'été,
Semble le refléter l'infini des lampes.

Et je voudrais
Courir, comme du temps de l'abeille, cherchant
Du pied la balle souple, car peut-être
Je dors, et rêve, et vais par les chemins d'enfance.

III.

I move forward then, up under the arch of a doorway.
The snowflakes whirl, erasing
The bound between outdoors and this room
Where the lamps are lit: but they are themselves
A kind of snow, that lingers
Between the height, the depth, of this night.
It's as if I stood on a second threshold.

And beyond, the same sound of bees
In the sound of snow. What they say,
The numberless bees of summer,
The infinitude of lamps seems to reflect.

And I would like
To run, as in the era of the bee, chasing
My rubber ball, because perhaps
I'm asleep, and dream, and follow the paths of summer.

IV

Mais ce que je regarde, c'est de la neige
Durcie, qui s'est glissée sur le dallage
Et s'accumule aux bases des colonnes
À gauche, à droite, et loin devant dans la pénombre.
Absurdement je n'ai d'yeux que pour l'arc
Que cette boue dessine sur la pierre.
J'attache ma pensée à ce qui n'a
Pas de nom, pas de sens. Ô mes amis,
Alberti, Brunelleschi, San Gallo,
Palladio qui fais signe de l'autre rive,
Je ne vous trahis pas, cependant, j'avance,
La forme la plus pure reste celle
Qu'à pénétrée la brume qui s'efface,
La neige piétinée est la seule rose.

IV.

But what I see before me, is hardened snow
That has crept across the tiles
And builds up against the columns' bases
Left and right, and far ahead into the shadows.
Absurdly I have eyes only for the curve
Drawn by this slush across the stone.
No name, no meaning. O my friends,
Alberti, Brunelleschi, San Gallo,
Palladio, who gesture from the other shore,
I won't betray you, however, I pass on,
The purest form remains
That which the raveling mist has penetrated,
The trampled snowdrift is the only rose.

Là où retombe la flèche

Where the Arrow Falls

Farhad Ostovani, White Mulberry. 30 x 30 cm. 2006.
Water color, pastel and pencil on paper.

I

Perdu. À quelques pas de la maison, cependant, à guère plus de trois jets de pierre.

Là où retombe la flèche qui fut lancée au hasard.

Perdu, sans drame. On me retrouvera. Des vois se dresseront de toutes parts sur le ciel, dans la nuit qui tombe.

Et il n'est que quatre heures, il y a donc encore beaucoup de jour pour continuer à se perdre—allant, courant parfois, revenant—parmi ces pierres brisées et ces chênes gris dans le bois coupé de ravins qui cherche partout l'infini, sous l'horizon tumultueux, mais ici, devant le pas, se resserre.

Nécessairement, je vais rencontrer une route.

Je verrai une grange en ruine, d'où partait bien une piste.

Appellerai-je ? Non, pas encore.

I.

Lost. Just a few feet from the house, yet hardly more than a stone's throw, or two or three.

Where the arrow falls, shot any which way.

Lost, without drama. Someone will find me. Voices will rise from anywhere under the sky, in the night that is falling.

And it is only four o'clock, there is still plenty of daylight for getting lost—walking, running sometimes, circling back—among these broken stones and gray oaks in the forest crisscrossed by ravines, which seeks the infinite everywhere, under the tumultuous horizon, although here, before my feet, it closes in.

Surely I'm going to find a path.

I'll see a ruined barn, from which a path once led away.

Will I call out? No, not yet.

II

Perdu, pourtant. Car il lui faut décider, presque à tout instant, et voici qu'il ne peut le faire. Rien ne lui parle, rien ne lui est plus un indice. L'idée même d'indice se dissipe. Dans l'empreinte qu'avait laissée la parole, sur ce qui est, l'eau de l'apparence déserte est remontée, brille seule.

Chaque mot : quelque chose de clos maintenant, une surface mate sans rien qui vibre, une pierre.

Il peut l'articuler, il peut dire : le chêne.

Mais quand il dit : le chêne—et à voix haute, pourquoi ? —le mot reste, dans son esprit, comme dans la main la clef qui n'a pas joué se fait lourde. Et la figure de l'arbre se clive, se fragmente et se rassemble plus haut, dans l'absolu, comme quand on regarde ces bossellements du verre qu'il y a dans d'anciennes vitres.

La couleur, rejetée sur le bord de l'image par le gonflement dans le verre. Ce qu'on appelle la forme troué d'un ressaut —démenti. Comme si s'était ouverte la main qui garde serrées couleurs et formes.

II.

Lost, all the same. For he must make a decision, at almost
every moment, and look, he can't do it. Nothing speaks
to him, nothing is a sign for him any more. Even the
idea of a sign fades away. In the footprint that speech
leaves behind, pressed on what is, the water of empty
appearance wells up, shines all alone.

Each word: something shuttered now, a matte surface
with nothing that resonates, a stone.

He can articulate it, he can say: oak.

But when he says: oak—and out loud, why?—the word
remains, weighs on his mind, as a key that didn't fit feels
heavy in the hand. And the shape of the tree splits, breaks
up, and reassembles higher, in the absolute, as when
one looks through those bosses in the glass of antique
windowpanes.

Color, thrown back to the edge of the image by the
swelling of the glass. What one calls the form, bevelled
around the edges—belied. As if it opened, the hand that
holds together colors and forms.

III

Perdu. Et les choses accourent de toutes parts, se pressent autour de lui. Il n'y a plus d'ailleurs dans cet instant où il veut l'ailleurs, si intensément.

Mais le veut-il ?

Et quelque chose accourt du centre même des choses. Il n'y a plus d'espace entre lui et la moindre chose.

Seule la montagne là-bas, très bleue, l'aide ici à respirer dans cette eau de ce qui est, qui remonte.

Familière pourtant cette impression d'une poussée qui s'exerce sur lui de par le dedans de tout. Hier, déjà, que de chemins trop abrupts vers le point de fuite, dans l'encre répandue des nuages ! Que de mots qui venaient d'il ne savait où, parmi les mots ! Que de ses jouets qui d'un seul coup n'étaient plus le petit damier ou les cubes couverts d'images mais le bois usé par le bord, la fibre qui perce la couleur.

On lui disait, de loin : Viens, et il n'entendait que cet éclaboussement du son qui se répand sur les dalles.

III.

Lost. And things rush in from every direction, throng around him. There is no longer any elsewhere, at this moment when he wishes so intensely for elsewhere.

But does he want it?

And something rushes in from the very center of things. There is no longer any space between him and the least thing.

Only the mountain over there, very blue, helps him to breathe here in this flood of what is, which is rising.

And yet it's familiar, this impression of a force that acts on him from the inside of everything. Yesterday, already, what paths there were, too steeply inclined towards the vanishing point, in the spilled ink of clouds! What words, which came from who knows where, among the clouds! What toys, his toys, which all at once were no longer the little checkerboard or cubes covered with pictures, but rather wood worn at the edges, where fiber breaks through color.

Someone would speak to him, from far away: Come, and he would only hear the spattering of sound that echoes off flagstones.

IV

Il se souvient qu'un oiseau avait marché devant lui tout un
moment quand c'était le chemin encore.

Il va droit, depuis deux minutes. Mais le voici arrêté par
de l'eau qui bouge parmi des souches. Il y a de la boue dans
cette eau claire, une sorte de poudre bleue qui tourne sur
soi là où le courant presque imperceptible frappe l'arête
brillante d'une roche.

S'il avait plu il retrouverait la trace de ses pas, mais la
terre est sèche.

Le sentier qu'il avait suivi laissait le soleil à sa gauche.
C'est là où il tournait qu'il y avait eu près du bord ces
trois pierres tachées de blanc, comme peintes.

IV.

He remembers that a bird walked ahead of him for
quite a while when the path was still there.

He has walked in a straight line, for two minutes.
But here he is, halted by the water that stirs
among tree stumps. There is some mud in this
clear water, a kind of blue powder that swirls
where the almost imperceptible current strikes the
shining ridge of a rock.

If it had rained, he could have retraced his
footsteps, but the earth is dry.

The path that he had followed kept the sun on
his left. Just where it turned there had been next
to the edge those three stones stained white, as if
painted.

V

Mais pourquoi gravit-il maintenant cette butte presque
escarpée, encore que les arbres y soient aussi serrés qu'en
dessous, le long d'étroites ravines ? Ce n'est sûrement pas
par ici que le chemin passe.

Et ce n'est pas de là-haut qu'il aura vue.

Ni pourra crier son appel.

Je le vois pourtant qui monte parmi les fûts, dans les
pierres.

S'aidant d'une branche basse quand il sent le sol trop
glissant à cause des feuilles sèches parmi lesquelles il
y a toujours ces cailloux roulant sur d'autres cailloux :
losanges de bord acéré et de couleur grise, tachée de rouge.

Je le vois—et j'imagine la cime. Quelques mètres d'à-plat,
mais si indistincts du fait de ces ronces qui atteignent
parfois aux branches. La même confusion, le même hasard
que partout ailleurs dans le bois, mais ainsi en est-il pour
tout ce qui vit. Un oiseau s'envole, qu'il ne voit pas. Un
pin tombé une nuit de vent barre la pente qui recommence.

V.

But why now is he climbing this rise, almost an escarpment, even though the trees here grow just as thick as down below, along the narrow ravines? It's certainly not this way that the path goes.

And it's not from up there that he'll have a view.

Nor be able to shout his appeal.

And nonetheless I see him climbing among the tree trunks, through the stones.

Holding on to a low branch when he feels that the ground is too slippery because of the dry leaves among which there are always pebbles rolling on other pebbles: rough diamond-shapes with sharp edges, gray in color, stained red.

I see him—and I imagine the summit. A few meters where the ground is flat, but quite indistinct because of those brambles that sometimes reach as high up as tree branches. The same confusion, the same randomness everywhere else in the woods, but then it's like that for all living things. A bird flies away, which he doesn't see. A pine tree that fell one windy night bars the slope upwards that begins again.

Et j'entends en moi cette voix, qui sourd du fond de l'enfance : Je suis venu ici, déjà—disait-elle alors—, je connais ce lieu, j'y ai vécu, c'était avant le temps, c'était avant moi sur la terre.

Je suis le ciel, la terre.

Je suis le roi. Je suis ce tas de glands que le vent a poussé dans le creux qui est entre ces racines.

And I hear that voice in me, which wells up from the depths of childhood: I've come here before—so the voice said—I know this place, I lived here, it was before time, it was before my own self on earth.

I am the sky, the earth.

I am the king. I am this heap of acorns that the wind swept into crevices among these roots.

VI

Il a dix ans. L'âge où l'on regarde les ombres se déplacer,
est-ce que par saccades ? et la déchirure dans le papier
des murs, et le clou planté dans le plâtre avec autour du
métal rouillé les infimes écaillements de l'incompréhensible
matière. S'est-il perdu ? En fait, il avance depuis
longtemps parmi de grandes énigmes. Il a toujours été seul.
Il s'est assis sur l'arbre tombé, il pleure.

Perdu ! C'est comme si l'au-delà que scelle le point de fuite
venait se pencher sur lui, et le touchait à l'épaule.

Lever les yeux, alors. Quand deux directions sollicitent
également, à un carrefour, le cœur bat plus fort et plus
sourd, mais les yeux sont libres. Ce soir, à la maison, qu'il
place des bûches sur le feu, comme on lui permet de le
faire : il les verra brûler dans un autre monde.

Qu'il parle, pour lui seul : les mots retentiront dans un
autre monde.

VI.

He is ten years old. The age when one watches shadows
shift, could it be in sudden leaps? And the ripping in the
paper of walls, and the nail implanted in plaster with,
around the rusted metal, tiny scalings of incomprehensible
matter. Is he lost? In fact, he has been moving forward
among great mysteries for a long time. He was always
alone. He sits down on the fallen tree, he starts to cry.

Lost! It's as if the far distance that the vanishing point
seals off had come to lean over him, and touched him on
the shoulder.

Open your eyes, then. When two directions beckon
equally, at a crossroads, your heart beats harder and yet
muted, but your eyes are free. This evening, back home,
if he sets logs on the fire, as he is permitted to do: he will
watch them burning in another world.

If he speaks, for himself alone: the words will resound in
another world.

Et plus tard, bien plus tard, de longues années plus tard,
seul, seul toujours dans sa chambre avec ce livre qu'il a
écrit : il le prendra dans ses mains, regardera les lettres
noires du titre sur le carton léger, teint de bleu. Il en
séparera quelques pages, pour qu'il soit debout sur la
table.

Puis il en approchera une allumette enflammée, une tache
brune puis noire va naître dans la couleur, s'y élargira, se
trouera, un liseré de feu clair en mordra les bords, qu'il
écrasera du doigt avant de redresser la brochure pour
réinscrire le signe à un autre endroit de la couverture.
Voici maintenant que tout un coin de celle-ci est tombé.
Le papier glacé, très blanc, de la première page, est apparu
au-dessous, atteint lui-même, jauni, par la chaleur.

Il pose le livre, il va garder en esprit, il ne sait encore
pourquoi, le mariage des phrases et de la cendre

And later, much later, long years later, alone, always alone
in his room with the book that he wrote: he will pick it
up in his hands, look at the black letters of the title on the
light cover, colored blue. He will separate a few of the
pages, so that it stands up on the table.

Then he will bring a lighted match close to it, a stain
first brown then black will begin to grow within the
color, become larger, pierce itself, a border of bright fire
will sink its teeth into the edges, which he will crush
out with a finger before righting the little book in order
to reinscribe the sign at another place on the cover. See,
now a whole corner of it has fallen off. The glossy paper,
intense white, of the first page, appears underneath, itself
stricken, yellowed, by the heat.

He sets the book down, he will preserve in memory, he
still doesn't know why, this marriage of words and ash.

VII

L'aboi d'un chien, qui a mis fin à sa peur. Le pilier du
soleil parmi les nuages, le soir. Les flaques que l'écolier
voit étinceler dans les mots, dans l'à venir de sa vie, quand
il pousse sa plume rêche dans l'enchevêtrement de la dictée
trop rapide.

Et toute branche devant le ciel, à cause des évasements,
des resserrements de sa masse. L'invisible qui là
bouillonne, comme la source au dégel, violente. Et les
baies rouges, parmi les feuilles.

Et la lumière, au retour; la flamme en quoi tout commence
et tout prend fin.

VII.

The barking of a dog, which finally put an end to his fear.
The pillar of sun-fire among the clouds, at evening. The
tiny pools that the schoolboy sees sparkle among words,
in the "to come" of his life, when he pushes his rough pen
into the tangle of a dictée read out too quickly.

And each branch against the sky, because of the
expansions, the contractions of its mass. The invisible
which boils up there, like a spring in winter's thaw,
violent. And the red berries, among the leaves.

And the light, at homecoming: the flame in which
everything begins and everything meets its end.

Afterword

Emily Grosholz

"Song, Rain, Snow:
Translating the Poetry of Yves Bonnefoy"

Around 1975, I read a book of Yves Bonnefoy's poems for the
first time, *Du mouvement et de l'immobilité de Douve*, and immediately
set my hand to translating some of them. In September 1977, I
attended his lectures on Baudelaire and Hugo at Yale University,
and then showed him some of my translations. He was
appreciative, we struck up a correspondence, and I got to know
him and Lucie Vines Bonnefoy when I spent half a year in Paris in
1981. I have been translating his poetry ever since; because his
sensibility seemed close to my own while his poetic habits were
very different, it was a challenging combination. At first, I dealt
with the affinity-and-distance by writing "versions," like Robert
Lowell, allowing myself a great deal of freedom in departing
from the original text. Here is one of those early translations,
published (much later) in the Autumn 2001 issue of *The Hudson
Review*, "The French Issue." The original poem appeared in *Hier
régnant désert* (1958) in the section "Le chant de sauvegarde."

À la voix de Kathleen Ferrier

Toute douceur toute ironie se rassemblaient
Pour un adieu de crystal et de brume,
Les coups profonds du fer faisaient presque silence,
La lumière du glaive s'était voilée.
Je célèbre la voix mêlée de couleur grise
Qui hésite aux lointains du chant qui s'est perdu

Comme si au delà de toute forme pure
Tremblât un autre chant et le seul absolu.

O lumière et néant de la lumière, ô larmes
Souriantes plus haut que l'angoisse ou l'espoir,
O cygne, lieu réel dans l'iréelle eau sombre,
O source, quand ce fut profondément le soir!

Il semble que tu connaisses les deux rives,
L'extrême joie et l'extrême douleur.
Là-bas, parmi ces roseaux gris dans la lumière,
Il semble que tu puises de l'éternel.

To the Voice of Kathleen Ferrier

All gentleness and irony converged
For this farewell of crystal and low clouds,
Thrustings of a sword played upon silence,
Light that glanced obscurely on the blade.

I celebrate the voice blended with gray
That falters in the distances of singing
As if beyond pure form another song's
Vibrato rose, the only absolute.

0 light and light's denial, smiling tears
That shine upon both anguish and desire,
True swan, upon the water's dark illusion,
Source, when evening deepens and descends.
You seem to be at home on either shore,
Extremes of happiness, extremes of pain.
And there among the luminous gray reeds
You seem to draw upon eternity.

Here Bonnefoy writes in a conscious modification of the conventions of nineteenth century French verse, four line stanzas where the syllable count is usually ten or eleven, occasionally the twelve-count of the alexandrine, though the smoothness of the lines gives the general impression of Baudelairean sonority. Likewise, he avoids full end rhyme, but instead ensures that the final two or three syllables of each line in a stanza present a great deal of mutual assonance and consonance, which again gives the impression of a diffuse rhyme and holds the stanza together in a way analogous to the aural unity conferred by full end rhyme: "couleur grise," "s'est perdu," "forme pure," "seul absolu," for example, in the second stanza.

My response was to write in iambic pentameter (not iambic hexameter, the English alexandrine). Because in general an Anglophone translator must use more words than are given to translate a French phrase, I had to leave something out here and there. I also used slant rhyme, in irregular patterns, a strategy less subtle than Bonnefoy's, but it was my wont to use slant rhyme with iambic pentameter. So without thinking much about it, I imposed my own prosodic habits on the poem. This was typical of most of my translations, until Larissa Volokhonsky brought it to my attention a few years ago, when we were translating poems by Olga Sedakova, whose free verse really couldn't be reduced to my own poetic proclivities. In the case of this poem by Bonnefoy, however, the imposition rested more lightly on the poem, because it was closer to the structure of the original.

But what did I leave out? The second stanza begins "Je célèbre la voix mêlée de couleur grise," which I render as "I celebrate the voice blended with grey," leaving out "couleur" and therefore a gentle play on, or echo of, "coloratura." The next three lines tell us more about the voice and perhaps also its "couleur grise," "Qui hésite aux lointains du chant qui s'est perdu," which becomes

"That falters in the distances of singing." This leaves out the clause that modifies "chant," "qui s'est perdu," and also, because I changed "song" to "singing," erases the perfect repetition of the word "chant" in the second and fourth line, which signals an important identity and difference. Indeed, this poem is built on repetitions and oppositions. I did manage to reproduce most of the repetitions (light, seem, gray, extreme), and most of the oppositions (light / obscurity, silence / singing, happiness / pain), with two important exceptions. I translated "espoir" as "desire," inaccurately, in order to reproduce (as I think now in retrospect) the original sound, since "hope" would have been difficult to insert musically into that line; and I lost the opposition between height and depth in the third stanza, leaving only the interplay between light and dark, tears and smiles.

In the last stanza, the gentle juxtaposition of "couleur" and "grise" in the first stanza, which isn't exactly an opposition but rather an uneasiness between noun and adjective, arises again in the "roseaux gris dans la lumière." Since I render that phrase as "luminous gray reeds," and since I erased the first juxtaposition by leaving out "color," that revisiting is also lost. The older I get, the more I have come to value the significance of repetition in poetry (as in life), what it creates and what it conveys; so I probably would translate this poem differently today. All the same, I'm fond of this translation of mine and find it, as a poem in English, beautiful. That's important, because the poem in French is also especially beautiful, especially sonorous, like the voice and song it celebrates. I have reproduced the many echoes of Baudelaire that I hear in it (whether or not the poet intended them), the vocabulary, the synaesthesia, the liquids and sibilance, the melancholy, the swan.

I also like some of my choices of vocabulary: "thrustings" for "coups profonds," "falters" for "hésite," "vibrato" as the noun that captures the verb "tremblât," "dark" for "sombre," "happiness" and "pain" for "joie" and "douleur." Except for the Italian "vibrato," I have used Anglo-Saxon words instead of the Norman English cognates, "hesitate," "somber," "joy," "dolor." Throughout the poem, Bonnefoy insists upon the tension between his notion of "présence," and the Platonic, otherworldly way of understanding the transcendence of art. One way to recreate that tension in English is to fold it into the vocabulary, so that more concrete, earthy Anglo-Saxon words are ranged beside the Norman English and Latin: "silence," "absolute," "illusion," "eternity." In general, when I translate Bonnefoy, I feel the pull of words with Anglo-Saxon roots especially strongly, sometimes, as here, to express something I find in the poem, and sometimes to create a counterpoint between his voice and mine.

Years later, forty years later in fact, I have finished translating Yves Bonnefoy's *Début et fin de la neige* suivi de *La où retombe la fleche*. In the meantime, as I mentioned above, after working with Larissa Volokhonsky on translations of a few poems by the Russian poet Olga Sedakova, I changed some of my habits as a translator. Here is a bit of what she wrote to me, which conveys the spirit of our exchange. (She first wrote out a translation-draft of the poem in English, I worked on it, and we discussed it, sometimes with Sedakova, until we were both satisfied.) "Here I am with my head full of ideas, which you may or may not share . . . In fact, it is just one idea. I firmly believe that in translating another person's text the first thing to do is to try to convey the spirit of the text as well the author's voice and its tone. It may prove to be impossible or only partly possible, but one at least has to try. The translator should allow another person's voice to speak through him or her. In a certain sense it is an exercise in humility, because through you another's voice comes to life in a different language. Of course one cannot efface oneself completely, and a translation always bears a translator's stamp. Now you and Olga Sedakova write very different poetry. Let us try and see how this difference can be diminished. First of all, there is, at least in this poem, an absolute absence of iambic pentameter. The rhythm and cadences are indicated by the length of the lines. Some lines are very short, some consist of just one word, which therefore bear strong semantic and rhythmic emphasis. Because she is not bound by the demands of the rhythm, the language is very terse, economical. In my literal translation I tried to follow her line breaks the best I could, and I think that as you work on your version you may want to look at the Russian text."

I had also been reflecting long and hard, in the meantime, on the importance of the poetic line and of repetition in a poem. Since I came to the conclusion that they are both central to the magic that a poem works, I had my own reasons for agreeing with Larissa Volokhonsky and so for trying harder to preserve them more faithfully in the translation. Moreover, speaking as a poet, I get tired of my own endless iambic pentameter and have looked for strategies to escape it sometimes, so translating the freer verse of Sedakova and Bonnefoy is then also good practice for me. At the same time, I have come to agree with Larissa Volokhonsky: one wants to lose as little as possible of the poet's voice.

Thus, I have gone about translating *Début et fin de la neige* in a different way. I have consulted the poet more often, and listened more attentively to his advice. Thus my translation of the poem "La Parure" from the first section of the book, entitled "La Grande Neige," respects Bonnefoy's line breaks almost exactly, except for two lines close to the end where the grammatical differences between French and English persuaded me to transpose the lines. I managed to reproduce the repetition of "neige" (as verb) and "neige" (as noun), of the root in "lumière" and "illuminée," and of "main."

However, I do translate by the single English word "gown" two distinct locutions in French, "robe de fête" and "parure," which is also the poem's title. I talked at length with the Bonnefoys about this word, and looked it up in many reference works: it means generally the whole outfit or costume that a woman would wear to a fancy event, gown and jewels. When English speakers (in for example a fashion magazine) want to convey this idea, they often use the French word! In the poem, however, the poet concentrates on the gown and the gown is itself bejeweled: lines 5–10 are devoted to its description. So I stayed with the word "gown." "La parure," by the logic of the poem, is also the snow, as well as the brightly lighted room into which the soul walks: both immortality and death.

Richard Lewontin has made the following illuminating observation about an organism and its environment: "Just as there can be no organism without an environment, so there can be no environment without an organism. There is a confusion between the correct assertion that there is a physical world outside of an organism that would continue to exist in the absence of the species, and the incorrect claim that environments exist without species... An *environment* is something that surrounds or encircles, but for there to be a surrounding there must be something at the center to be surrounded. The environment of an organism is the penumbra of external conditions that are relevant to it because it has effective interactions with those aspects of the outer world." He adds, "organisms not only determine what aspects of the outside world are relevant to them by peculiarities of their shape and metabolism [and activities], but they actively construct, in the literal sense of the word, a world around themselves" (*The Triple Helix*, Harvard University Press, 2001, pp. 48 and 54).

To illustrate this point, he observes that birds make nests and people build houses and wear clothes, but in addition to these constructions, every metabolizing organism lives in a self-produced atmosphere, a micro-environment that insulates it from the outer air. "In normal circumstances, it is the warm, moist, self-produced shell that constitutes the immediate space within which the organism is operating, a space that is carried around with the individual just as a snail carries around its shell." The imaginative conceit of this poem is that the beautiful snow is an environment for the soul, as a dress is for the body or—in an extended sense—a room. (If a brightly lit, gilt and mirrored ballroom is a setting for a beautiful young girl, then it is—in an extended sense—part of her "parure.") The crystalline snow, with its flowering snowflakes, is very beautiful, but also lethal for a human organism. To step into its immortality is to succumb to death.

Think then, in the light of these reflections of a great philosophical biologist, how odd a human being is. Our environment is not only constructed by our own insulating layer of air, our clothes and houses, but also by our extraordinary minds. We also construct a social environment that is safe and encouraging by maintaining the rituals of friendship, eros, neighborliness and citizenship; we enact and maintain our familial and professional worlds. Moreover, we are aware of not only our own environment but those of most other living things, and the vast reaches of reality where the orders of magnitude far surpass or undercut our own, where stars, snowflakes and atoms live, precipitating their own vast and minute environments. Beyond even those realms, our minds reckon with not merely the here-and-now, but its thoughtful frame, the negated, the universal, the conditional and unrealized, the past and future, space itself, and indeed the infinite.

One aspect of the paradox and power of mind, is that we can try to imagine reality without ourselves, *without* mind. The metaphysics of Democritus, developed into an ethical system by Epicurus and a great epic by the Roman poet Lucretius, carries out the strange thought experiment of imagining a universe where the only real things are atoms in the void; thus *De Rerum Natura* is a counter-example to Aristotle's famous dictum that poetry is the imitation of human action. For *De Rerum Natura* dissolves both plot and character in the reduction of every thing to a rain of atoms, and to illusion all that we hold most dear and fearful. To enter the metaphysics of Democritus or the poetry of Lucretius is to take on a whirl of snowflakes for a dress, a house, an environment, into which we disappear, deathless but undone.

Yet paradoxically it is Lucretius who tells the tale, Bonnefoy who inverts it into a lyric reflection on the snows of New England, we who read it. We are still here! Or as Descartes put it, almost lost in his own skeptical vortex, "*Cogito . . . Sum.*" And let us add: "*Canto.*" Moreover, the song remains for others to take up, "shadows / Who walk off laughing, one / In red wool coat and mittens."

I talked to the Bonnefoys at length about the word "emmitouflée" as well: it means "bundled up," the way one bundles up a child to go out sledding, in a hat, mittens, scarf, snowpants, and jacket, and of course the gender is feminine. I couldn't figure out how to convey the latter, hoping that the couple "two shadows" would suggest a man and a woman; and I decided to convey the former by letting the part stand for the whole. In the context of Bonnefoy's *oeuvre*, the phrase "une laine rouge" echoes for me the phrase "une robe rouge" or just "une robe" which so frequently turns up in his poems, usually flung across a chair, a splash of color, a sign of eros, an affirmation of human warmth. We are still here! Thus "une laine rouge" is opposed to the ghostly "parure" of the snow, and the laughter of the one who walks away from the beautiful cold chamber, the tomb, disrupts its silence.